JOHN THOMPSON'S
EASIEST PIANO COUR

FIRST CHILDREN'S SONGS

Arranged by Christopher Hussey

ISBN 978-1-5400-3483-0

EXCLUSIVELY DISTRIBUTED BY

WILLIS MUSIC

HAL•LEONARD®

7777 W. BLUEMOUND RD. P.O. BOX 13819
MILWAUKEE, WISCONSIN 53213

Visit Hal Leonard Online at
www.halleonard.com

Contact Us:
Hal Leonard
7777 West Bluemound Road
Milwaukee, WI 53213
Email: info@halleonard.com

In Europe contact:
Hal Leonard Europe Limited
42 Wigmore Street
Marylebone, London, W1U 2RN
Email: info@halleonardeurope.com

In Australia contact:
Hal Leonard Australia Pty. Ltd.
4 Lentara Court
Cheltenham, Victoria, 3192 Australia
Email: info@halleonard.com.au

Twinkle, Twinkle, Little Star

Traditional

The Wheels on the Bus

Traditional

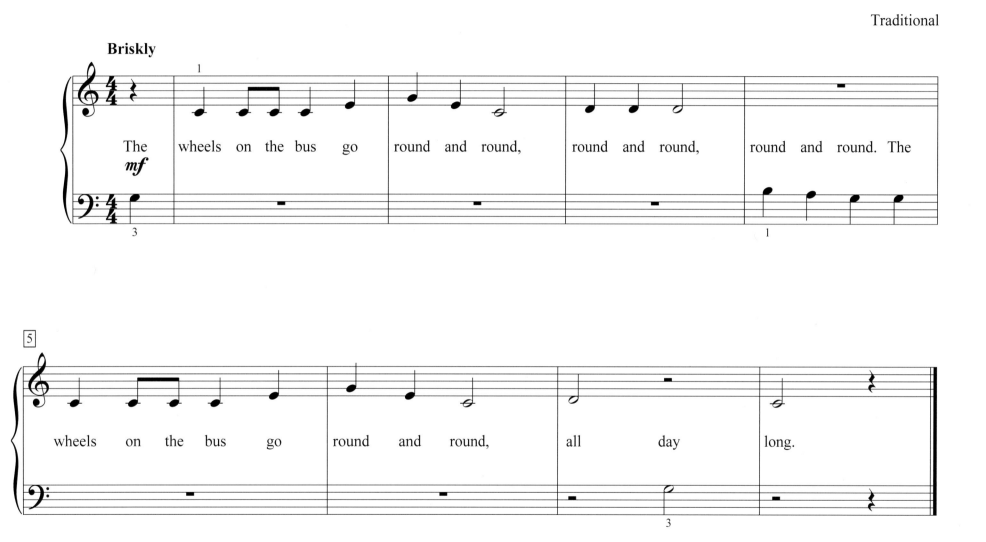

Baa, Baa, Black Sheep

Traditional

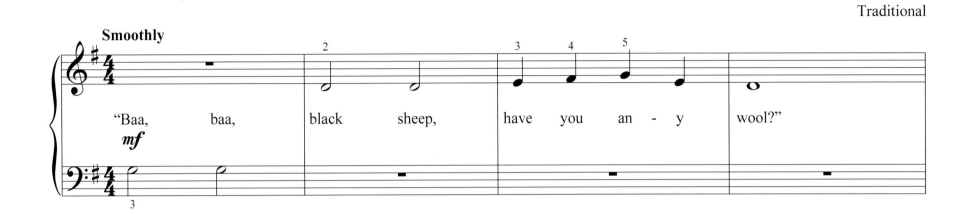

"Baa,   baa,   black   sheep,   have   you   an - y   wool?"

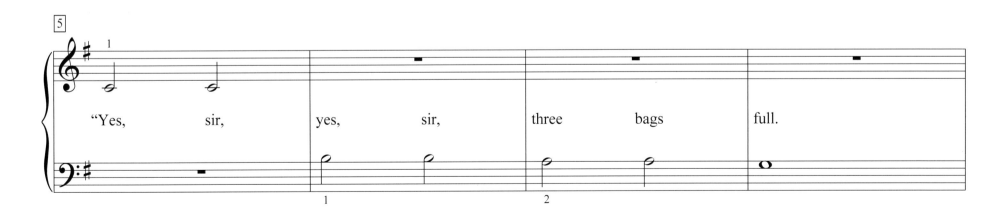

"Yes,   sir,   yes,   sir,   three   bags   full.

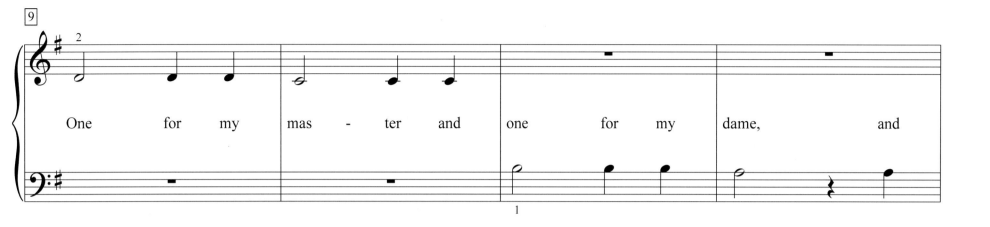

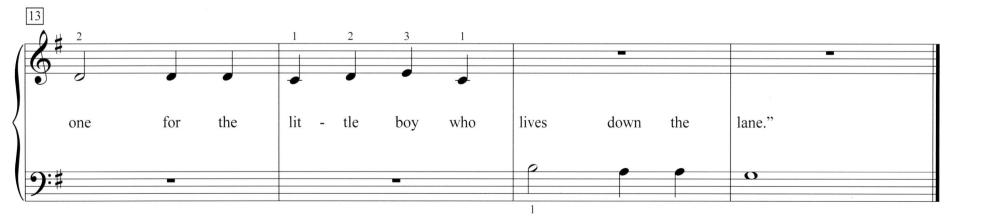

She'll Be Coming 'Round the Mountain

Traditional

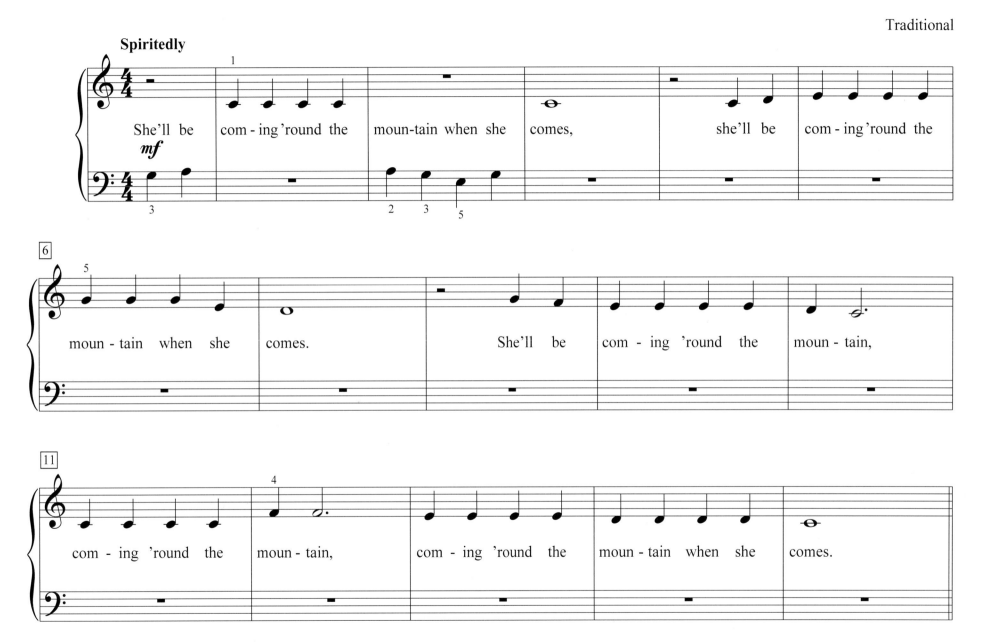

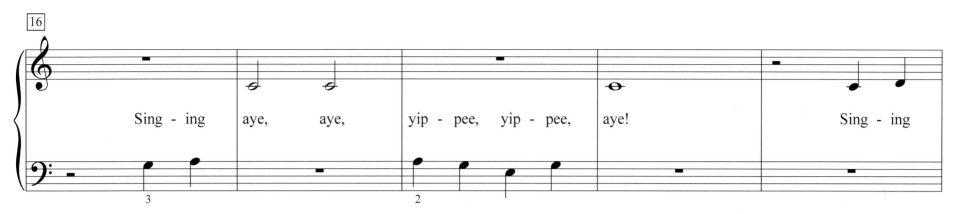

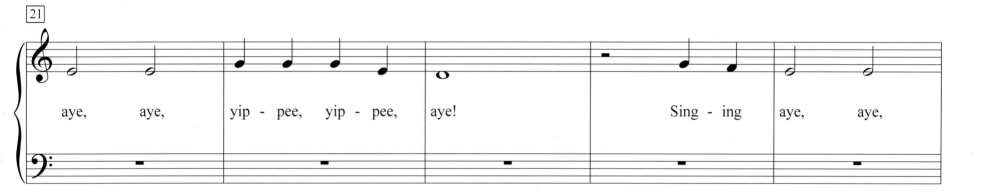

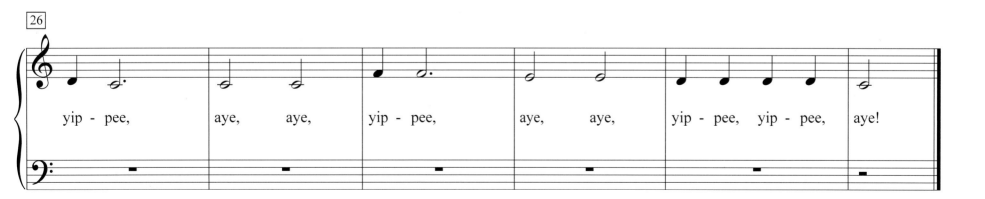

A-tisket, A-tasket

Traditional

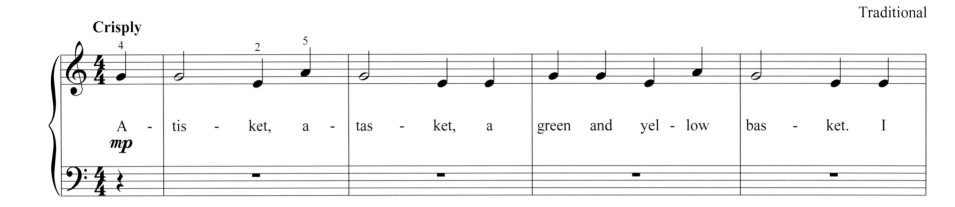

A - tis - ket, a - tas - ket, a green and yel - low bas - ket. I

wrote a let - ter to my love and on the way I dropped it. I

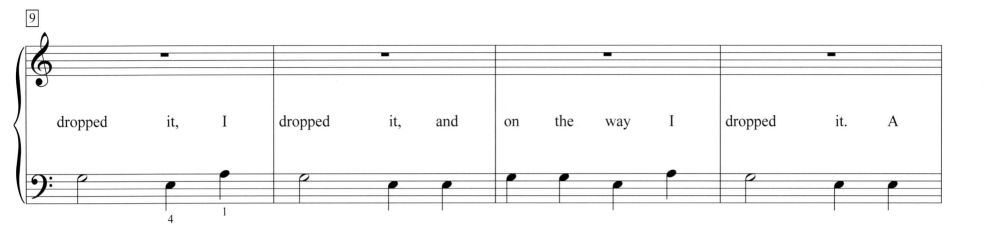

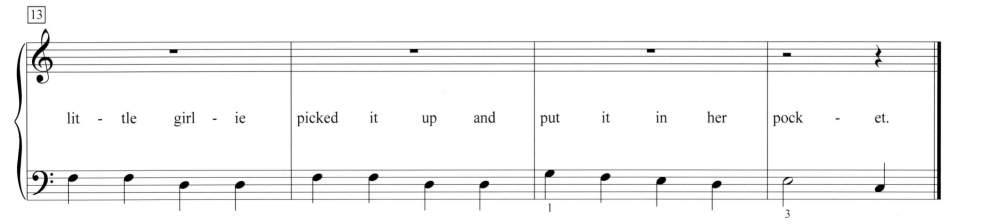

Michael Finnegan

Traditional

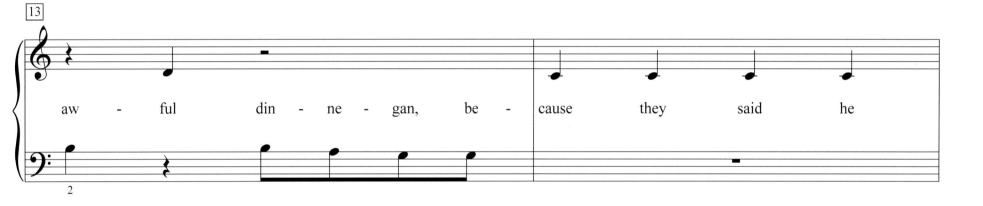

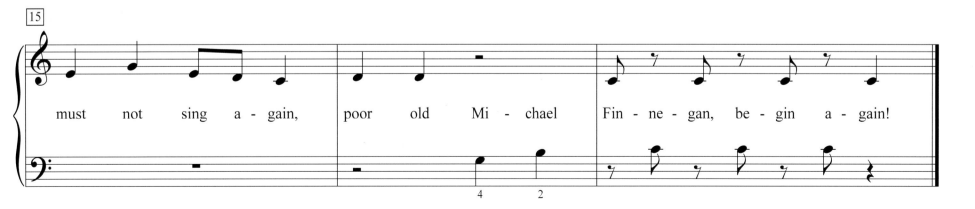

Three Blind Mice

Traditional

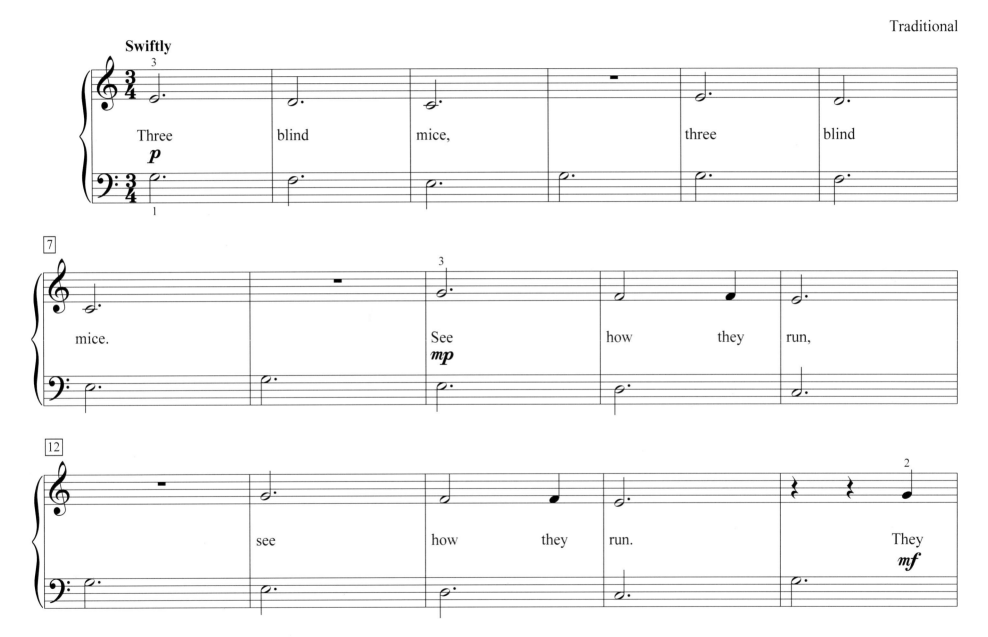

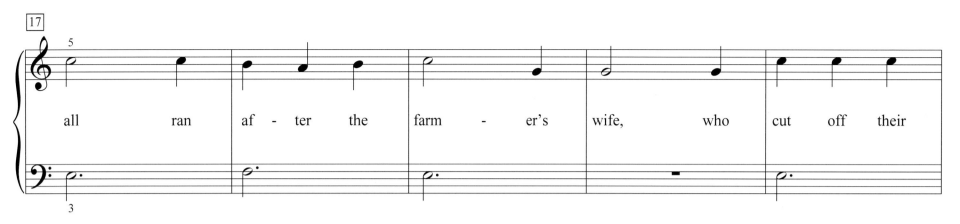

all ran af - ter the farm - er's wife, who cut off their

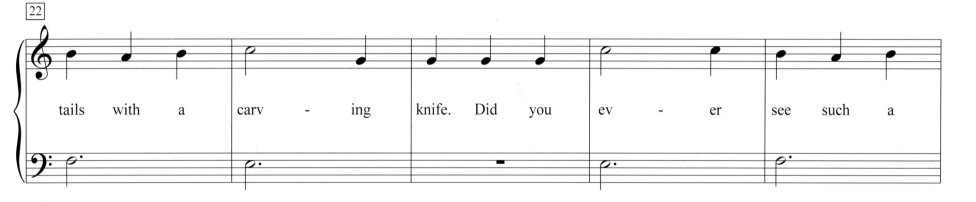

tails with a carv - ing knife. Did you ev - er see such a

sight in your life as three blind mice?

Polly, Put the Kettle On

Traditional

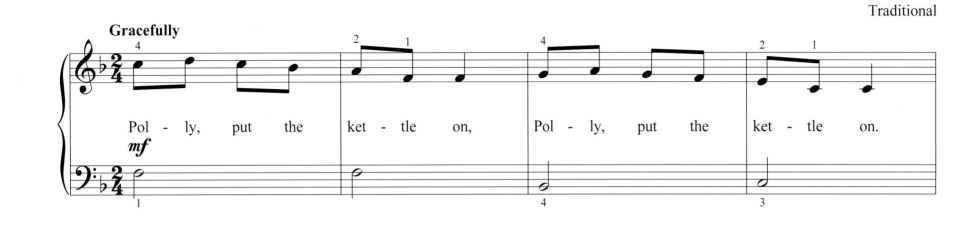

Polly, put the ket - tle on, Polly, put the ket - tle on.

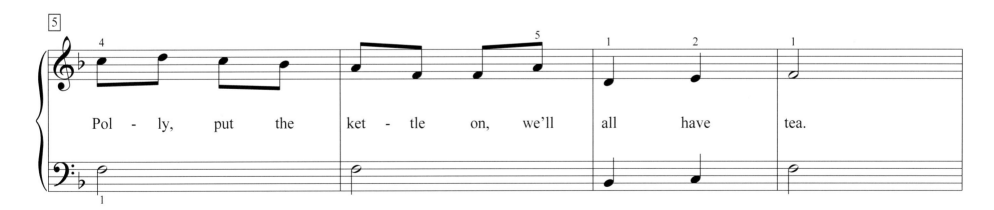

Polly, put the ket - tle on, we'll all have tea.

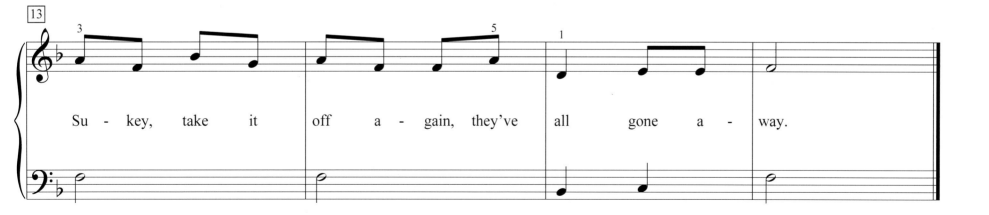

Old MacDonald Had a Farm

Traditional

Old Mac-Don-ald had a farm, E - I - E - I - O! And

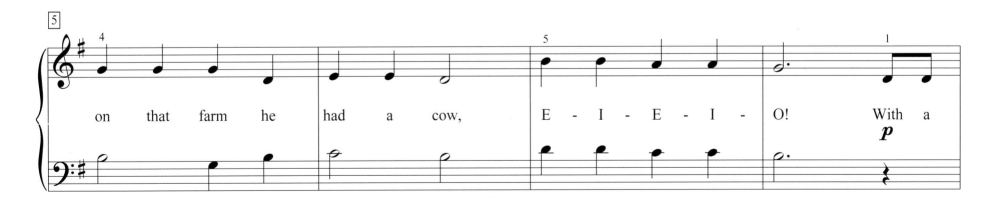

on that farm he had a cow, E - I - E - I - O! With a

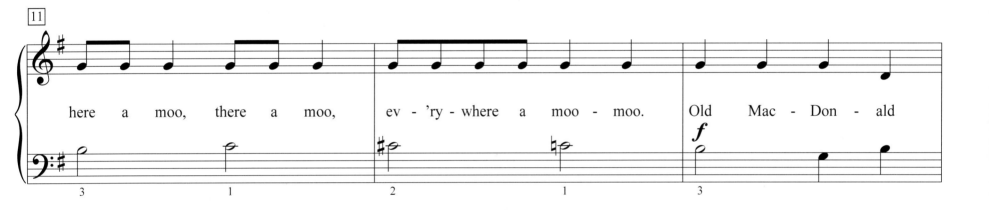

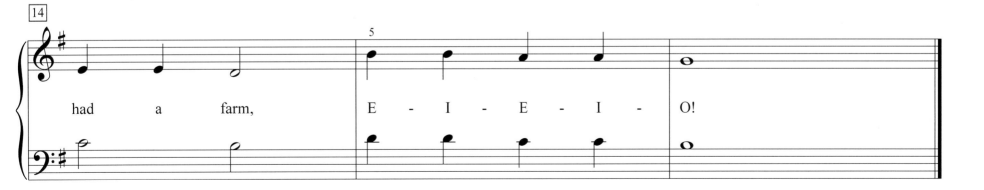

The Muffin Man

Traditional

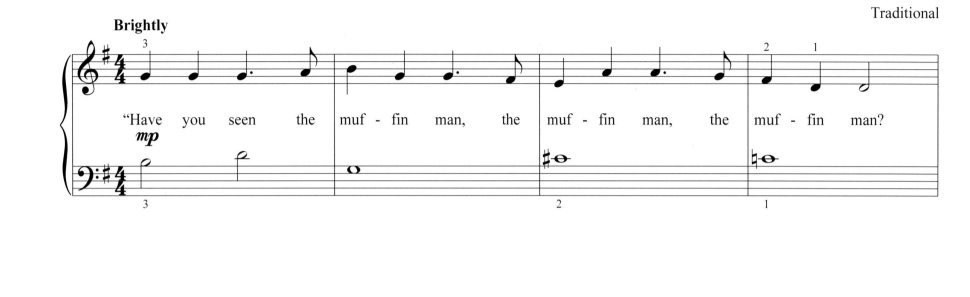

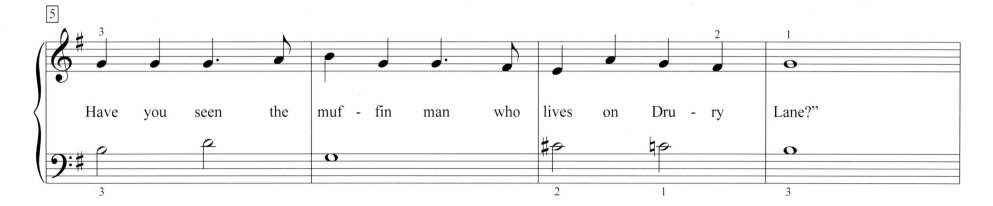

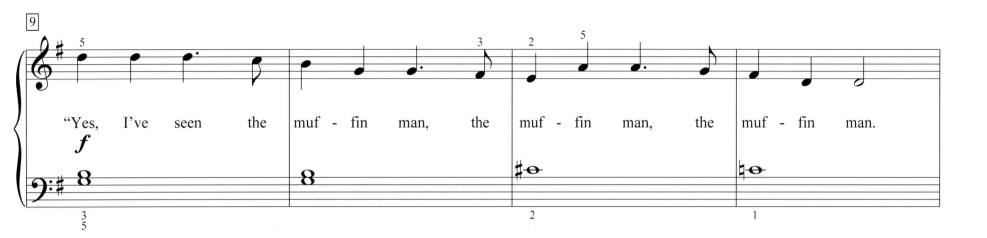

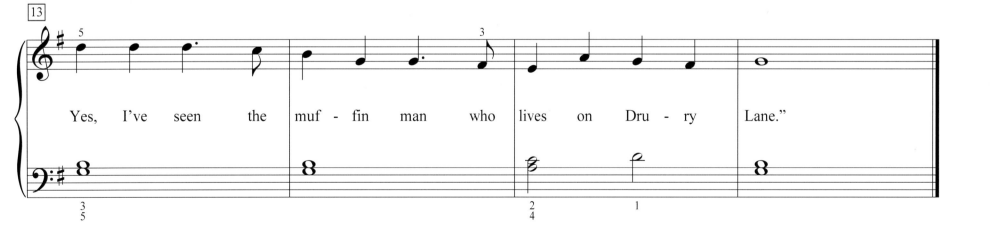

Row, Row, Row Your Boat

Traditional

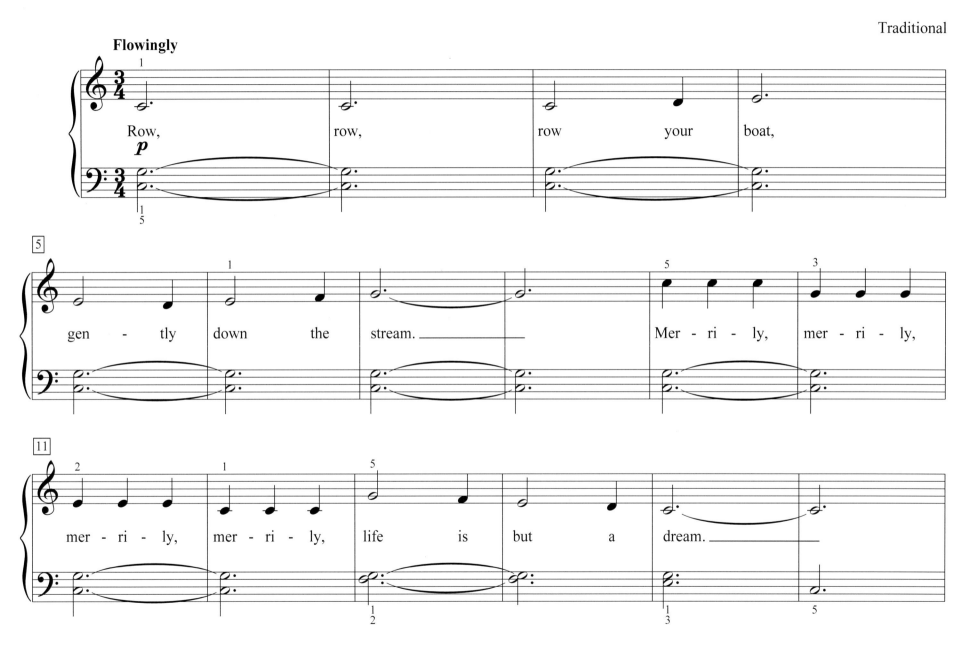

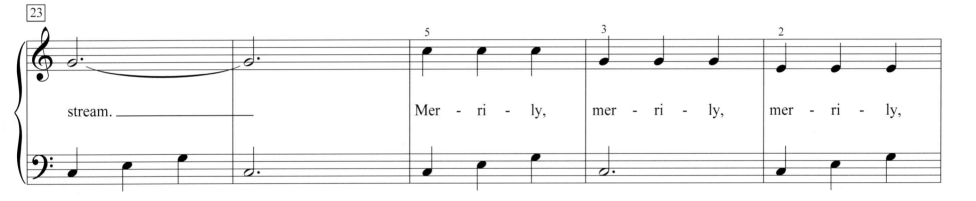
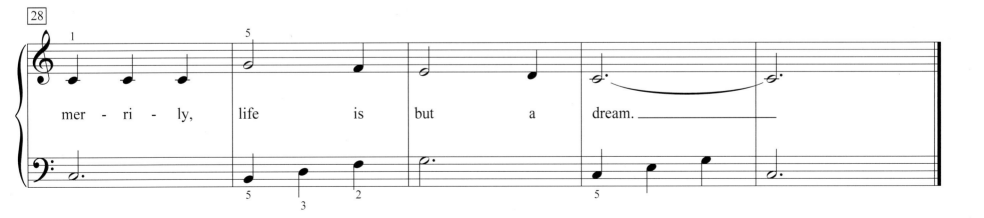

Polly Wolly Doodle

Traditional

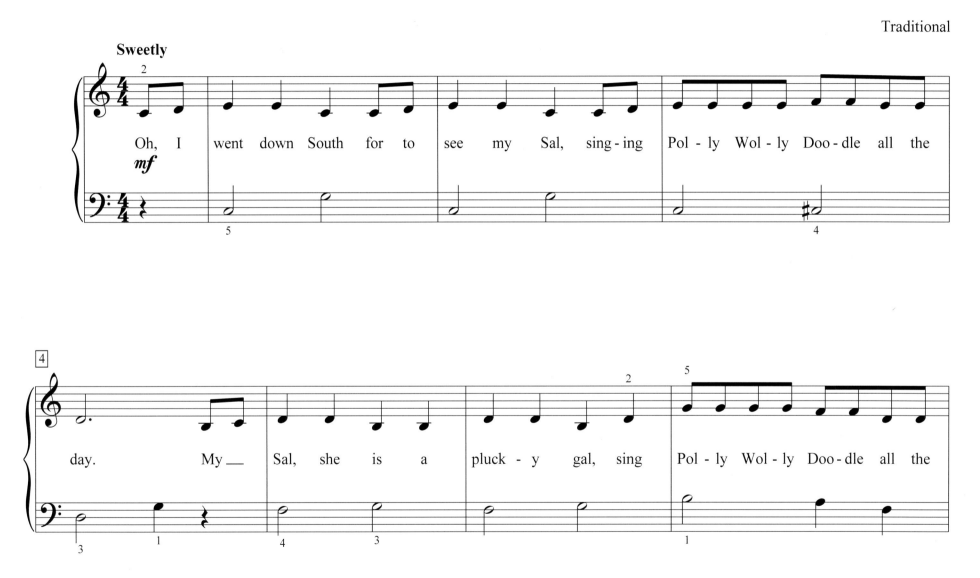

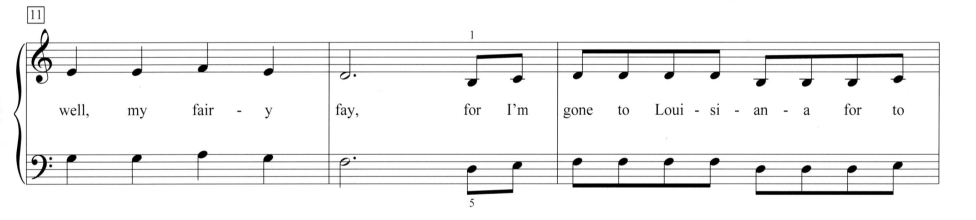

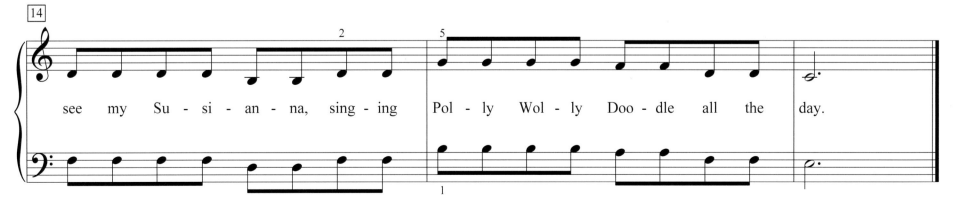

Alice the Camel

Traditional

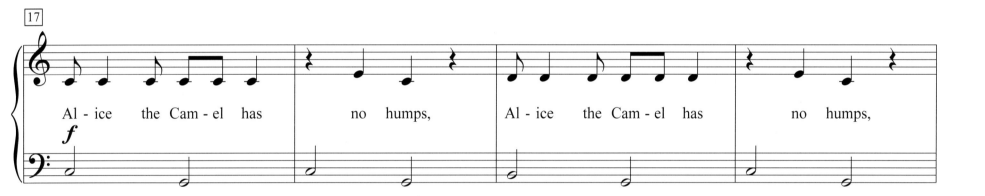

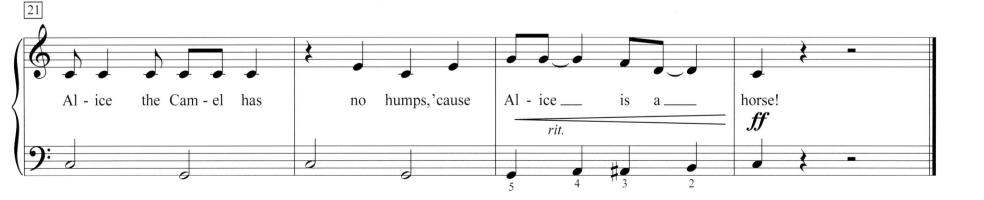

Pop! Goes the Weasel

Traditional

All a - round the mul - ber - ry bush, the mon - key chased the wea - sel. The

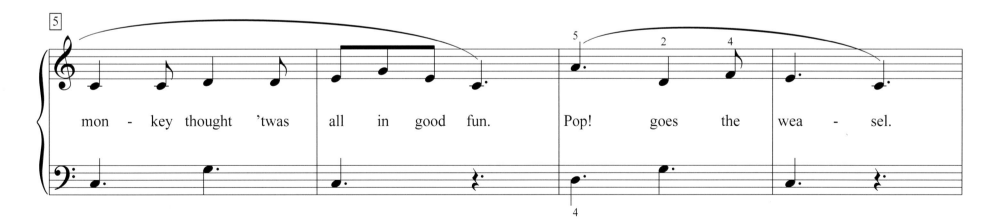

mon - key thought 'twas all in good fun. Pop! goes the wea - sel.

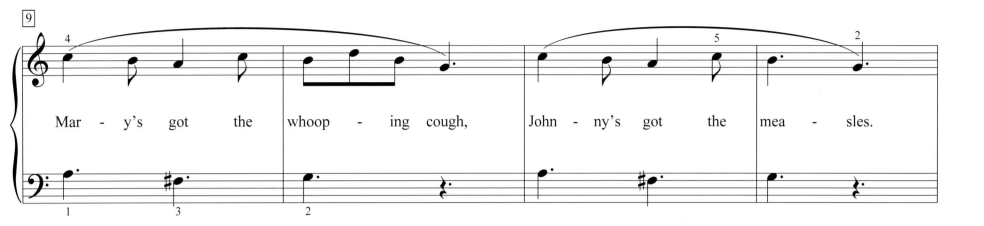

Mar - y's got the whoop - ing cough, John - ny's got the mea - sles.

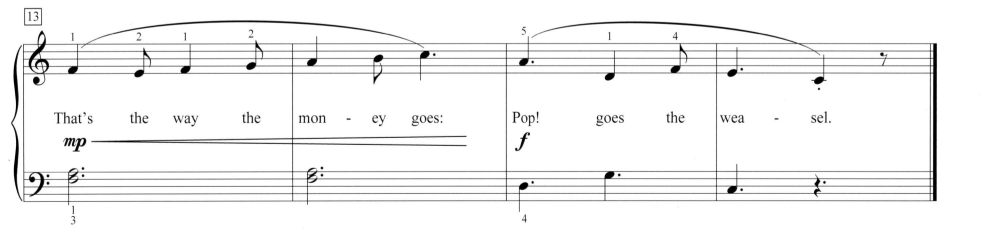

That's the way the mon - ey goes: Pop! goes the wea - sel.

The Animal Fair

Traditional

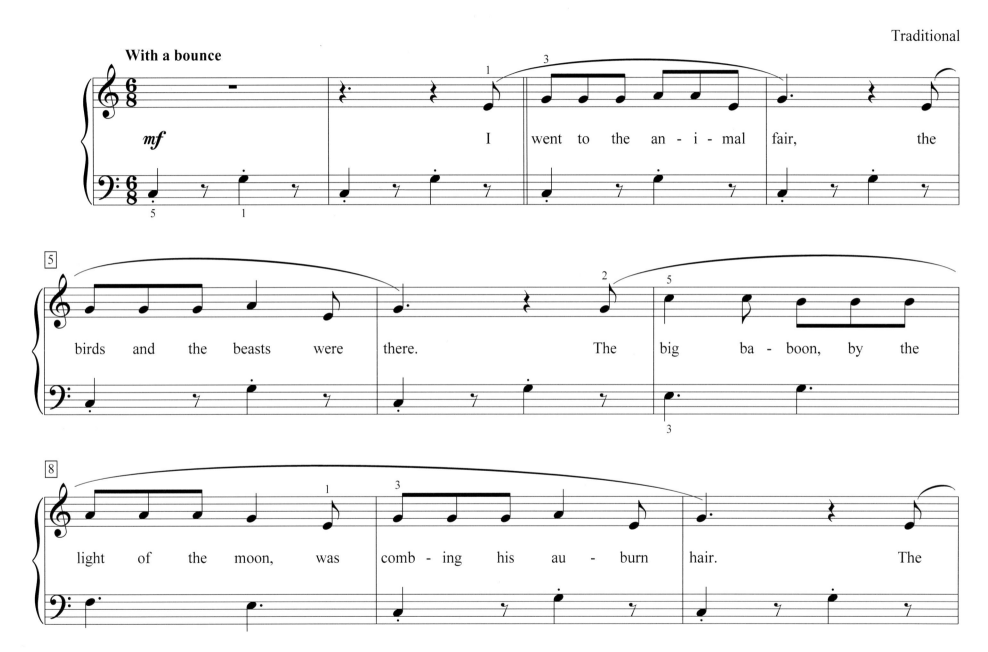

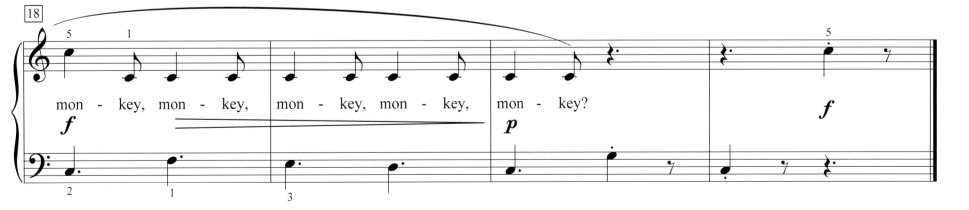

Happy Birthday to You

Words and Music by Patty S. Hill
and Mildred Hill

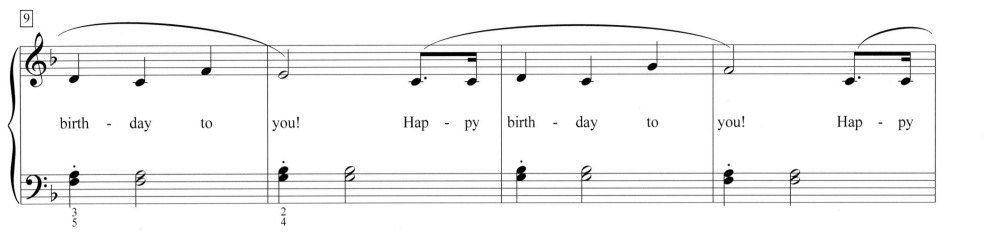

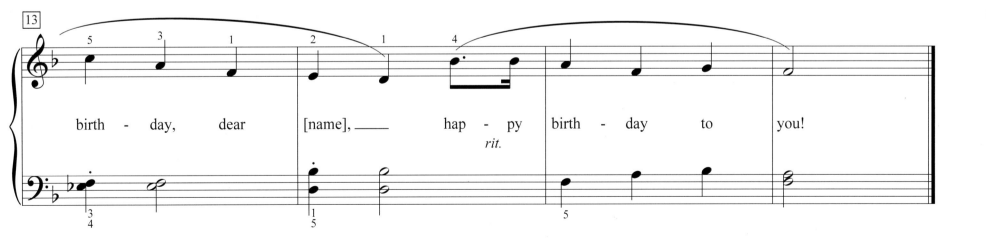

EASIEST PIANO COURSE
Supplementary Songbooks

Fun repertoire books are available as an integral part of **John Thompson's Easiest Piano Course**. Graded to work alongside the course, these pieces are ideal for pupils reaching the end of Part 2. They are invaluable for securing basic technique as well as developing musicality and enjoyment.

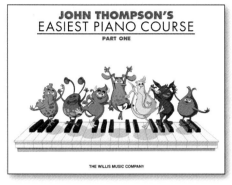

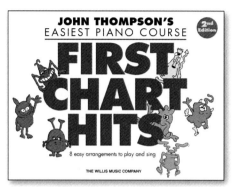

John Thompson's Easiest Piano Course

00414014	Part 1 – Book only	$6.99
00414018	Part 2 – Book only	$6.99
00414019	Part 3 – Book only	$7.99
00414112	Part 4 – Book only	$7.99

First Beethoven *arr. Hussey*
00171709.................................... $7.99

First Chart Hits – 2nd Edition
00289560.................................... $9.99

First Disney Songs *arr. Miller*
00416880.................................... $9.99

Also available:

First Children's Songs *arr. Hussey*
00282895 ....$7.99

First Classics
00406347....................................$6.99

First Disney Favorites *arr. Hussey*
00319587 ....$9.99

First Mozart *arr. Hussey*
00171851....................................$7.99

First Nursery Rhymes
00406229....................................$6.99

First Worship Songs *arr. Austin*
00416892....................................$8.99

First Jazz Tunes *arr. Baumgartner*
00120872.................................... $7.99

First Pop Songs *arr. Miller*
00416954.................................... $8.99

First Showtunes *arr. Hussey*
00282907.................................... $9.99

WILLIS MUSIC

EXCLUSIVELY DISTRIBUTED BY
HAL•LEONARD®

Prices, contents and availability subject to change without notice.   *Disney Characters and Artwork TM & © 2019 Disney*   View complete songlists and more songbooks on **www.halleonard.com**

0819
474